Keiko & the Crow

Judy Lane & Robert Maughan, Jr.

AuthorHouse™
1663 Liberty Drive, Suite 200
Bloomington, IN 47403
www.authorhouse.com
Phone: 1-800-839-8640

First published by AuthorHouse   6/2/2009

ISBN: 978-1-4343-9529-0 (sc)

Library of Congress Control Number: 2008912216

Printed in the United States of America
Bloomington, Indiana

This book is printed on acid-free paper.

"Who would have imagined a special friendship between a dog and a crow? *Keiko and the Crow* tells the sweet story that developed over an extended period of time. Judy's observation of this unique relationship is through the eye of a scientist and delivered as an artist in a compelling, tender, and entertaining story for all."

— Art Wolfe

This Book Belongs to:

~~~~~~

Dedicated to the brilliant Siberian Husky Iko and all the
Siberian Huskies we have loved over the years.

Photography, Photo collages, and Graphic Art by Judy Lane
Excellent Graphic Artist Assistance by Robert Harrison

"Shared experience is the basis of all communication." (unknown)

Cautionary note:
The one thing I worry about
Is that a child might let a fenced Siberian out.
So, if you have this breed,
Please proceed,
But know that our Siberians do walk on a lead.
And if you plan to purchase this breed,
Then this story is a must-read!

Front and Back Cover: How many crows and canines can you find?

Once there was a husky puppy named Keiko,

and his brother's name was Sekiu.

Northwestern Huskies they would be,

enjoying their life by the sea.

For Siberian Huskies, the snow, wind, and cold

provided the basis of many a tale told.

But this is an unusual story —

one that will now unfold.

Keiko and Sekiu loved to play with each other,

especially since they were brothers.

They would test their strength

with a good wrestle

and sometimes ended up twisted

like a pretzel!

Keiko and Sekiu loved
to run on the beach —
up and over the driftwood,

preparing for other
special talents
by developing their
balance.

And they loved to talk to each other

with their mouths close together.

Then soon enough,

they'd be howling like wolves,

practicing their singing skills —

with the sound echoing

throughout the hills.

Being Siberian Huskies,

Keiko and Sekiu loved to experiment

by trying some unusual games,

with all that energy to tame!

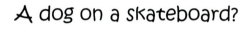

A dog on a skateboard?

That was a sight to see!

Or running in place inside a barrel?

A very strange place for a husky puppy to be!

And Keiko definitely got a thrill

slipping

down

a

slide,

but was still full

of energy inside!

So Keiko, true to his breed,

just had to run ...

and run ...

and run,

with amazing speed!

Back and forth he'd go,

this funny puppy named Keiko!

Once in awhile, Keiko would stop long enough to dig a hole ...

but could one hole become one hundred?

"With some time and little effort," Keiko said.

He dug one hundred and one

just because it was so much fun.

He dug the next because

of Siberian Husky stubbornness!

Before the end of his hole-digging spree,

Keiko had made his total one hundred and three!

So in the course of
an afternoon,
his backyard looked like the
surface of the moon!

A yard that was once full of flowers
now looked like it had been hit by a meteor shower!

Keiko, feeling his power,

dug another ...

and another.

And then blamed it on his brother!

While claiming it wasn't his fault,

Keiko just had to do a somersault ...

which at least brought the hole digging to a halt!

Keiko's extra energy

might be viewed as his only flaw,

but if he were hooked up to a dogsled,
it wouldn't be at all!

One day, Keiko really wanted to play.

As much as he tried

to interest Sekiu in a game,

Sekiu said he wanted to rest,

thank you all the same!

So with a big yawn,

Sekiu curled up

as if he'd sleep until dawn.

The choice between a walk or a nap?

Well, for Keiko

that decision was a snap!

Keiko decided not to stay;

instead he

set out on a beautiful winter's day.

As Keiko found his way

down through the park that day,

he got to explore every

boulder and tree,

and meet every other animal and bird,

as well as you and me.

He also met a very nice girl

named Cheriè.

And, as always with Keiko,

hugs and kisses were free!

In seeking out another playmate,

it was a family of crows

he intended to find

— he hoped they wouldn't mind,

since crows have a job to do,

and that is finding

plenty of food!

However, Keiko had noticed

that they, too, loved to play,

like soaring on a windy day.

Keiko saw one crow fly out over the bay,

and he watched in wonder at the wave-skimming display.

Then, looking up,

he noticed the crow family

roosting in their favorite tree.

Keiko could hear them talking and talking away,

apparently with quite a lot to say!

But these crows were high in the air,

out over the water,

or way up in a tree,

and these were all places Keiko knew he couldn't be!

So Keiko kept exploring—investigating places high and low.

By looking under the water in a stream,

maybe he'd find the fish of his ancestral dream!

r he'd climb

way up

on a big tree stump.

hen, hanging on by his tippy toes,

naybe he'd launch himself off,

just like the crows!

Again feeling all that extra energy to spend,

he decided to wander back down to the shore,

and start digging some more!

When Keiko concentrated on his dig,

he found the hole would get really, really big!

With a husky's determination,

deeper and deeper he would go,

and less and less of Keiko would show!

On this day, one young Northwestern crow sought Keiko out at last.

While watching with his family, this crow had noticed and followed Keiko in the past.

Crows are known to remember certain people and animals, too.

With a curious interest in what they do,

Crows can even make up a call or two.

You might not have considered talking to a crow,

but some crows of this Northwestern wood

mimicked people's words just because they could!

Now everyone knows that a crow and a dog might not get along.

So could they really play or share or even sing a song?

After all, as long as their cousin, the raven,

has lived near wolves, this has been true.

But would it be so for these two?

So, as Keiko was having some fun

digging deep into the sand,

the young crow landed nearby,

took it all in,

and came up with a plan!

And as the crow watched, with great intent,

Keiko dug up some treasures,

just like a present sent.

Softly, the crow called,

"K .... ko,

K ... ko,

K ... ko".

Having heard it before,

he repeated this puppy's name,

getting the sound of it exactly the same!

But since Keiko was so very, very busy digging, at first he didn't realize

that this crow was talking!

And much to his surprise,

this crow was talking to *him.*

The crow watched closely as all the bugs tumbled out,
and while the sand was flying here and there and all about,
the crow moved a little closer:
two hops forward, one hop back!
A war of instincts made the crow unsure.
But the lure of a free meal?
That had great appeal!

Finally, the crow moved closer still—with his funny sideways step.

He grabbed a bug

or two or three,

and then hopped back.

And thanked the husky for the tasty snack!

Keiko looked up and smiled, and made his puppy's play bow

—a friendly invitation for all to see,

making *this* crow his playmate to be.

So a strange new dance developed on that beautiful, magical day

between this native Northwestern crow

and the husky puppy named Keiko.

And while they both

wanted to stay,

at the end of this special day,

each had to go their own

separate ways.

(Tired at last)

THE

END

Special thanks to

Susan Callahan, *owner of Galena Creek Kennels and breeder*

of these confident, intelligent little beings named Keiko and Sekiu.

Art Wolfe, *for taking the time to look at my artwork*

—and suggesting that I write a story!

And of course, my Mother, **Peggy Blackwell,**

for her unfailing support and active listening to all my husky (and crow) stories over the years!

To learn more about fascinating crows and ravens, please consult
In the Company of Crows and Ravens by John M. Marzluff and Tony Angell, Yale University, 2005

The Math Instinct — Why You're a Mathematical Genius (Along with Lobsters, Birds, Cats, and Dogs)
by Keith Devlin, Thunder's Mouth Press, 2005

Finally, I am forever grateful to the two crows, Crooked Feather Girl and Bold Boy, who revealed their intelligence as well as their observation and math skills and for their choice to share part of their lives with us.

Crooked Feather Girl

There was a crow
I came to know.
And I've come to believe
That she knew me.

One crooked feather
Is the only way
That I could tell her
From all the others.

So on those days
That our paths crossed
And the timing was just right,
She and I would go together a ways,
Usually just before night …

—By Judy Lane

CPSIA information can be obtained
at www.ICGtesting.com
Printed in the USA
409897LV00001B/1